A journey through
THE PEAK DISTRICT

EMERGENCY
999

DAVID SPARES SAUL'S LIFE

SMALLDALE

JARROLD

THE PEAK DISTRICT

It is doubtful whether any other region in Britain has such a variety of scenery, in a relatively small area, as the Peak District. The Dark Peak, an inverted horseshoe of sandstone and shales, covers three-quarters of it, mostly in the north. The White Peak fills the middle of the horseshoe, covering the south and centre of the Peak in carboniferous limestone.

The difference between these two areas is remarkable. The northern part, the Dark Peak, is craggy, wild, windswept heather and bilberry moorland, offering a haven for climbers, experienced walkers, grouse and mountain sheep. The southern part, the White Peak, has light-green turf, a gentle landscape with villages in the typical English style of cottages and a church grouped around a village pond or green. There are steep-sided dales where the rivers sometimes vanish into the porous rocks and caverns to emerge again several miles downstream.

Evidence of human life in the Peak goes back a long way. The oldest monuments, Neolithic burial chambers, were made by the first Peak settlers who arrived from continental Europe around 3000 BC. Five Wells, near Taddington, is the highest such tomb in Britain, at over 426 metres (1,400 feet). The most impressive Neolithic monument is Arbor Low, and there are Bronze Age remains in Stanton Moor associated with the nearby Nine Ladies Stone Circle.

The Saxons, a long time later, left little visible evidence, but the region was first called 'Peac-land' in Anglo-Saxon times, probably from the Old English *peac*, meaning 'hill'. This may explain why a region called the Peak District has

so few peaks. It has high places that rise over 600 metres (2,000 feet), but they are somewhat featureless and flat-topped and definitely not peaks.

The most extensive monument of the Norman Conquest is Peveril Castle and the town of Castleton, which it overlooks. The Middle Ages saw a great agricultural expansion. There was a vast increase in sheep and wool production, much of it directed from outside the Peak by monasteries. The wealth that wool generated helped to fund the building of churches such as those at Bakewell and Tideswell, and the stone walls that are such a feature of the Peak District today began to be erected at this time, to control the sheep which grazed the hillsides. Another attractive legacy of the prosperity of the Middle Ages can be seen in the fine manor houses such as the halls at Eyam,

Tissington, Hartington and North Lees, near Hathersage.

The Peak District National Park was created in 1951, the first in Britain, and is now one of the most visited in the world. Recreational facilities include cycle tracks on disused railway lines, industrial mueums, river canoeing, cavern exploration, stately homes and a cable-car railway, to name but a few. This book gives a taste of the many delights to be sampled in the Peak District, which are too varied to be covered completely in a few pages.

1 The view towards Kinder Reservoir
from Kinder Scout, Derbyshire

THE NORTHERN PEAK DISTRICT

The northern part of the Peak District is the rounded part of the inverted horseshoe that makes up the Dark Peak; the bare and open Pennine Way goes north from near the base of its highest point, Kinder Scout. The landscape is wild, wet, windy and wonderful. There are intriguing signs of ancient civilisations, for example, Carl Wark, near Hathersage, is built upon an easily defended rocky knoll and is probably of Iron Age origin. Remains of the largest and most impressive hill-fort, thought to pre-date the Iron Age, cap the summit of Mam Tor, the rest of it having disappeared down the unstable hillside. There are other notable examples at Combs Moss, near Chapel-en-le-Frith and Ball Cross, near Bakewell.

Nearer to our own time, the Roman Empire left behind signs of its occupation. In the Dark Peak the Romans built a fort at Navio, near present-day Brough, a 2-acre site that probably housed a garrison of 500 men to defend the Roman lead-mining concerns in the Peak. Another fort, Ardotalia, just outside Glossop, was connected to Navio by a road that ran over the peat bogs of Bleaklow and Kinder Scout. It is partly exposed along the section known as Doctor's Gate and runs beside the Snake Pass.

In recent years the landscape in parts of the Dark Peak has been dramatically altered by the flooding of valleys to create reservoirs, to supply Derby, Nottingham, Sheffield and Leicester with drinking water. Howden, Derwent and Ladybower reservoirs, in the Derwent Valley, are probably

the best known, but altogether there are fifty or so in the Peak. They are very popular with birdwatchers and fishermen, and much trouble has been taken to build purpose-made trails and paths, to landscape the banks and to provide public facilities. The popularity of the reservoirs is reflected in the fact that traffic management schemes, car parks and picnic areas have been created to ensure that a gentle stroll can be taken beside the water at any time.

The geological formations of Castleton make it a place rich in interest. Sited at the junction of the White Peak limestone and the Dark Peak grits and shales, it is surrounded on three sides by dramatic hills, caves and gorges. Three of the show caves for which the town is renowned are situated in the unusual and spectacular

gorge of Winnats Pass. Blue John and Treak Cliff mines have yielded a mineral called Blue John, a beautiful banded fluorspar, since at least the seventeenth century, but only Treak Cliff has a viable source today. The caves have wonderful, massive formations of stalactites, but the finest examples of Blue John in the world can be seen in the Ollerenshaw Collection.

Wild, heather-clad moorland in the Dark Peak is only ever a half-day's ramble, or a half-hour by car, from the gentle tree-shaded dales, rich in wild flowers and bird-song, to be found in the White Peak.

2 Kinder Downfall on the western edge of Kinder Scout plateau

3 Kinder Scout plateau is the highest point
in the Dark Peak, at 636 metres (2,088 feet)

4 'Shivering Mountain', or Mam Tor, is so-called
because the striped rock is made up of alternating
layers of soft, impervious shale and porous harder
grits, that slide over one another when wet

5 Edale is a valley containing five hamlets and is a major walking
centre. The Pennine Way footpath stretches 400 kilometres
(250 miles) from here to the Scottish Borders

6 The miles of Peak District drystone walls, so attractive and 'natural' looking, are just one example of human alteration of the environment to suit farming needs

THE MASS TRESPASS ONTO KINDER SCOUT STARTED FROM THIS QUARRY 24TH APRIL 1932

7 The moors of Kinder Scout and Bleaklow were jealously guarded for grouse-shooting, and in 1932 walkers trespassed to defy the landowners

8 One starting point for the Pennine Way is in Edale at the base of Kinder Scout

9 The Snake Pass, now the A57, very closely follows an old Roman road between forts at Brough and Glossop. It became a pack-horse route before being adopted as a road by Telford in 1821. It climbs to 512 metres (1,680 feet) before descending into Glossop

10 Parts of the Snake Pass are across open moor, such as Doctor's Gate which is a superb footpath. It was named after Dr John Talbot, vicar of Glossop from 1494 to 1550, who used it to cross the moors here

11 Old Glossop, the original gritstone village that visitors to Glossop often miss, lies to the east of the main town centre. The parish church, old market square and lovely seventeenth-century cottages contrast with the 'new' town built in the nineteenth century for the growth of the cotton industry

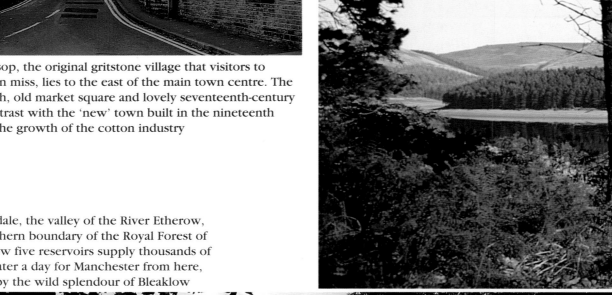

12 Longdendale, the valley of the River Etherow, was the northern boundary of the Royal Forest of the Peak. Now five reservoirs supply thousands of gallons of water a day for Manchester from here, overlooked by the wild splendour of Bleaklow

13 Towards the end of the nineteenth century the large cities of Derby, Nottingham, Leicester and Sheffield required regular water supplies. A chain of three reservoirs was built in the sparsely populated, narrow upper Derwent Valley. Howden Reservoir is one of them

14 The construction of dams and reservoirs and the planting of conifers in the upper Derwent Valley have created an artificial landscape; yet it is a very attractive one in which leisure activities can be pursued, as here on Ladybower Reservoir

15 Froggatt Edge, above the Derwent Valley, forms part of an almost unbroken line of crags that extends for 19 kilometres (12 miles) along the eastern rim of the Derwent Valley and provides superb views, excellent walking routes, and opportunities to try out rock-climbing skills

16 Several of the twenty-nine arches of the Penistone
Viaduct. By road from the market town of Penistone
it is easy to travel to the start of the Pennine Way

17 The building of the Derwent Reservoir in 1916 certainly
did not detract from the attractiveness of the area – the dam
is flanked by woodland that covers the gentle slopes

18 Holmfirth, made popular by the television series *Last of the Summer Wine*, is also famous for the saucy seaside postcards produced before the First World War, on display in the Holmfirth Postcard Museum

19 Stanage Edge, the highest part of the impressive gritstone edge, is very popular with climbers and hang-glider pilots. It can be approached by car from below, north of Hathersage

20 From Higger Tor, near Hathersage, there are splendid views. Carl Wark, an ancient hill-fort thought to date from AD 500 to 600, lies to the east of the town, Stanage Edge to the north and the River Derwent to the west

21 Carl Wark, a hill-fort above Hathersage, was built upon an easily defended rocky knoll and is probably of Iron Age origin

22 Charlotte Brontë visited Hathersage before writing *Jane Eyre*. She may subsequently have used the area as a model for the setting of her novel; Higger Tor is pictured here

23 Hathersage churchyard, high above the village, is said to contain the grave of the legendary Little John, Robin Hood's right-hand man; when the grave was opened in 1784 a thigh-bone for a man 2 metres (7 feet) tall was found

24 Winnats Pass, a spectacular steep gorge near Castleton, is a site of Special Scientific Interest and is owned by the National Trust

25 Castleton was a Norman town built in conjunction with Peveril Castle, which overlooks it

26, 27 The Normans left few visible reminders of their rule in the Peak District, but Peveril Castle, built as an administrative centre and hunting lodge for the Royal Forest of the Peak, is an exception. It was built by William Peveril, supposedly an illegitimate son of William the Conqueror

28 Three of the show caves for which Castleton is renowned are in Winnats Pass. The stone in this Blue John table, in the Ollerenshaw Collection, came from the Treak Cliff workings

29 Tours can be taken through the Treak Cliff Cavern; they pass through Fossil Cave, the eerie Witch's Cave, Fairyland with its grotto of delicate stalactites, and the Dream Cave, shown here

30 An autumn view from Treak Cliff, which is the only viable source of Blue John today

The remains of a crushing circle mark Odin
[M]ine, the area's oldest recorded lead mine

32 The approach to Peak Cavern, whose
entrance is about **15** metres (**50** feet) high
and nearly **30** metres (**100** feet) wide

A Canadian otter in natural surroundings
[at t]he Chestnut Centre between Castleton
[and] Chapel-en-le-Frith

The eighteenth-century mine
[at S]peedwell Cavern is entered
[by] boat along a floodlit
[un]derground canal

35 The imposing classical dress of Lyme Hall conceals a Tudor mansion – the owner in the 1720s, Peter Legh, employed an Italian architect to 'bring it up to date'. Inside, the sixteenth-century mansion reappears, and the contents reveal the long history of Lyme and the Legh family who owned it for 600 years. Now owned by the National Trust, it contains tapestries and furniture of outstanding quality, including early Chippendale chairs

THE SOUTHERN PEAK DISTRICT

The White Peak covers the greater part of the southern Peak District. The eastern and western sides of the area are the precipitous gritstone edges of the Dark Peak. To the east, Stanage, Millstone and Curbar edges are all close to good roads and easily reached by foot or by car. In the west, the Roaches, Ramshaw and Windgather rocks, equally accessible, are more broken but no less impressive, and favoured by rock climbers.

This southern area is much gentler than its northern neighbour. There are trails following the beds of old railways available to walkers, cyclists and horse-riders and beautiful dales to be explored. Most famous is Dovedale (so beloved of Izaak Walton, author of *The Compleat Angler*, in the seventeenth century) but there are many others, some of which are National Nature Reserves. The Nature Conservancy Council, the National Trust and the Derbyshire Wildlife Trust manage and protect the old meadows and woodlands where the variety of trees includes ash, elm, hazel and hawthorn, yew, bird cherry, field maple and buckthorn.

The rivers Manifold, Dove, Lathkill and Wye run through the White Peak, in places through almost perpendicular gorges formed during the Ice Age. These gorges are edged with

expanses of bare, gleaming white rock. In places the limestone has been formed into hills and thin pillars or needles, such as the spectacular series in Dovedale that includes Ilam Rock, Pickering Tor and Tissington Spires.

Sheep-farming and lead-mining were the mainstays of the medieval Peakland economy and, in the southern Peak District, fine mansions such as Haddon Hall and the splendid and palatial Chatsworth were built by prosperous local landowning families. Many of the villages in this area still carry out the custom of well dressing – once an ancient thanksgiving ceremony for the precious gift of water on the dry limestone, it now has strong religious associations.

During the Industrial Revolution the Peak District gave the world its first water-powered cotton mill. The spa town of Buxton became even more popular with the coming of the railways; it is now well-known as a cultural centre.

From rock-climbing and fossil-fossicking to orchestral concerts and stately homes, the Peak District has something for everyone.

36 Fernilee Reservoir's outstanding beauty is, perhaps surprisingly, very largely artificially made

37 Buxton is one of the highest towns in England – over 300 metres (1,000 feet) above sea-level, and one of the oldest spas in the country; in the late 1700s it became a second Bath. Nowadays it has the assured air of a place whose purpose is to entertain visitors

38 The fifth Duke of Cavendish began to establish Buxton as a
fashionable spa in the 1780s, and he had the sweeping Crescent
built close to the original St Ann's Well, which is open daily
throughout the season

39 The source of Derbyshire's River Wye is in Poole
Cavern, a spectacular limestone cave in which the
stalactites and stalagmites are illuminated to display the
subtle colourings. A visitor centre has displays relating
the cavern and Buxton Country Park which surrounds

40 The Monsal Trail, an old railway-track route, runs almost from Buxton to Bakewell, passing by the old station at Miller's Dale

41 The majestic Monsal Viaduct crosses the River Wye. The superb View is one of the delights of the Monsal Trail which passes over it

42 To find this lovely stretch of riverside walking in Monsal Dale follow the signs for the dale on the Monsal Trail. The path crosses a footbridge over the River Wye, goes alongside the river, under the viaduct and past the weir

43 The ancient custom of well dressing may have started during the Black Death as a thanksgiving for survivors escaping the plague through the purity of the waters

44 Annual well dressing ceremonies are held in many villages in Derbyshire. Village wells are decorated with tableaux (usually depicting Biblical themes) made from flowers, ferns, mosses, leaves and bark

45 Eyam (pronounced 'Eem') is a pleasant village with a grim history. In 1665 the plague arrived via a box of London cloth. The villagers put themselves in quarantine to prevent its spread

46 The fine manor houses of Tissington, Eyam Hall (seen here), Hartington and North Lees near Hathersage, were all built by prosperous landowning families in the Middle Ages

47 The stocks at Eyam seem insignificant when balanced against the tragedy and courage of the villagers in the plague year, when many sacrificed themselves to prevent other villages from being infected

48 The Riley graves are a memorial to seven members of one family who fell victim to the plague within the space of eight days

49 The Plague Cottages, where the plague first arrived in the village, stand near the church. The one in which the first death occurred is marked

50 Curbar Edge is part of the magnificent gritstone
escarpment along the eastern rim of the Derwent Valley.
It offers exhilarating walking and glorious views

51 Chatsworth – home of the dukes of Devonshire – is one of England's great houses, and is open to the public during the summer months

52 The most gifted artists, architects and craftsmen are represented in the contents and building of Chatsworth House. The gardens, too, contain treasures, including the Emperor Fountain whose magnificent jet of water is powered by natural pressure

53 The thirteenth-century bridge over the Wye at Bakewell was built originally for pack-horses and is one of the oldest in England

54 The small market town of Bakewell is popularly regarded as the 'capital' of the Peak District and contains some very old, interesting buildings

55 Few elements of the old Saxon church remain in the present church at Bakewell, but there are several Saxon carvings and stone fragments

56 The Saxon sculptured cross standing in Bakewell churchyard may have been used as a wayside preaching cross

57 The renowned Bakewell Pudding was the result of a happy mistake by a hotel cook who put jam underneath, instead of on top of, the filling

58 'The Stonehenge of the North', Arbor Low near Monyash, is the Peak's major prehistoric monument. The stones were probably upright when the henge was constructed around 2000 BC

59 Neglect is sometimes beneficial, as Haddon Hall shows. It is one of the finest medieval manor houses in the country because it was abandoned from 1640 until the early 1900s (thus escaping any Georgian or Victorian alterations), when the ninth Duke of Rutland began a thorough restoration

60 Magpie Mine's nineteenth-century lead-mine remains are the best preserved of their type. Like other Derbyshire lead mines it has had a chequered history which is told in the Mining Museum, Matlock Bath

61 The High Peak Trail is one of the excellent Peak District routes built on old railway lines for cyclists, walkers and horse-riders

62 The valley of the River Bradford can be reached by numerous alleyways and tracks from the old lead-mining village of Youlgreave

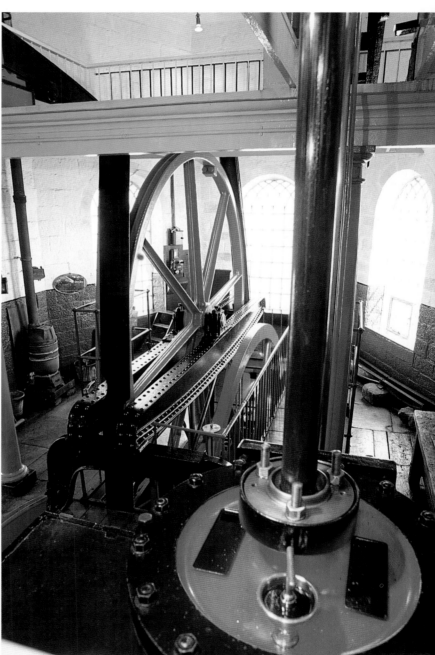

63 Occasionally the engine in Middleton Top Engine House is reawakened and although it is now run on compressed air it still suggests the power it had. A visitor centre tells the story of the railway and the engine house

64 The imposing fifteenth-century tower of Youlgreave church, which is one of the village's many historic buildings. At the end of June, Youlgreave's renowned well dressing can be seen

65 The Cork Stone stands on Stanton Moor, an isolated island of millstone grit in a sea of softer rocks, where there is a dense concentration of Bronze Age remains. The rungs were set into the stone in Victorian times and many feet have scaled it since

5 Not far from the Cork Stone, in a birch wood, is the Bronze Age
Nine Ladies Stone Circle. It is some 15 metres (50 feet) across and
may once have been a burial ground of some importance

67 'There are things as noble in Derbyshire as Greece or Switzerland', wrote Byron of Matlock Gorge. The cable-car ride from the foot of High Tor, across the steep-sided gorge to the Heights of Abraham, is spectacular

68 The Pavilion at Matlock Bath, which was once a popular spa town and is now a centre for fun and visitor attractions

69 Some Peak District rivers, such as the Derwent at Matlock Bath, are popular for canoeing

70 Richard Arkwright built the first water-powered cotton mill at Cromford in 1771

1 Horse-drawn barges still operate in summer from the once busy wharf on the Cromford Canal. A little further along the towpath, at High Peak Junction, the wharf and railway workshops have been carefully restored

72 Cromford was the first town in Britain built purposely to house factory workers. Arkwright's cotton mill (shown opposite) employed more people than were available locally, so cottages, a hotel, a chapel, a lock-up and a market place were constructed

73 The stepping stones across the River Dove join Staffordshire and Derbyshire

74 Dovedale is one of the most visited parts of the Peak, and Reynard's Cave one of its most well-known features

75 The River Dove inspired the literary partnership of Izaak Walton and Charles Cotton, co-authors of *The Compleat Angler* in 1653

76 The view from the mouth of Thor's Cave, the most spectacular feature of the Manifold Valley, is one of the great sights of the Peak

77 The Church of the Holy Cross in Ilam Hall Country Park is a village church which dates back to the thirteenth century. The oldest relics are three Anglo-Saxon crosses, one of which is in the grounds of the hall

Ilam Hall was rebuilt in the nineteenth century by Jesse Watts-Russell who built the model village of Ilam

79 The National Trust owns Ilam Hall Country Park, which is open to the public all year round

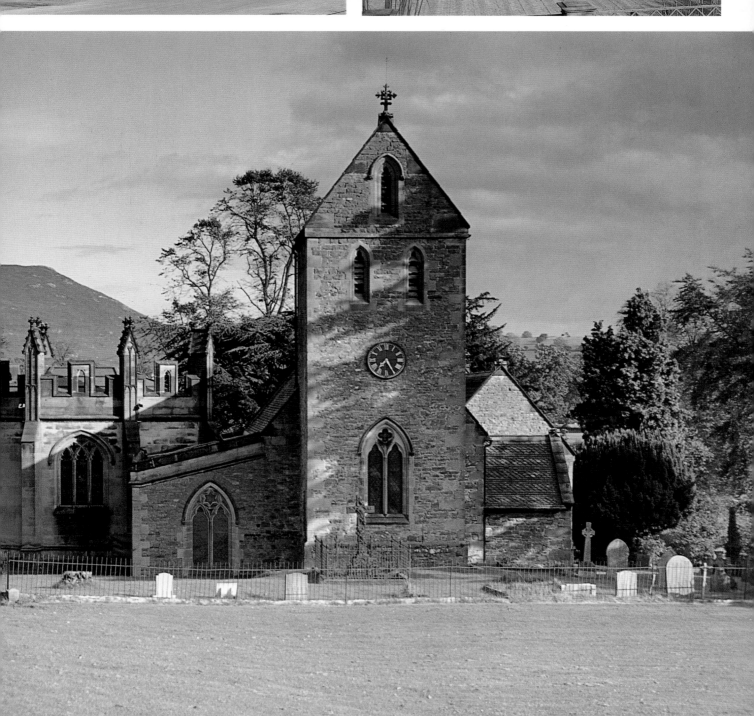

80 Rock-climbing at Hen Cloud; some of Britain's most famous climbers have begun their careers in the Peak District

82 Hen Cloud is part of the impressive rocky western arm of the horseshoe of grit that surrounds the White Peak. It is seen here from the Roaches, which probably derives its name from the French word for rocks – *roches*

1 The jagged Ramshaw Rocks are part of the gritstone rmation surrounding the White Peak in which the mous 'Winking Eye Rock' dominates. The centre of e basin formed by the rocks was partly filled with al-bearing measures with which local farmers would y to increase their meagre livings

83 When it was completed, the mansion of Alton Towers was the largest private house in Europe. Now a leisure park, almost a third of which is under cover, its entertainments are varied enough to please everyone